With Love From Jerusalem

A Good Friday Worship Service

FRANKLIN A. DVORAK
PAUL J. WECKLE
DANIEL THOMPSON
ANNETTE THOMPSON

C.S.S. Publishing Co., Inc.

Lima, Ohio

WITH LOVE, FROM JERUSALEM

9017 / ISBN 1-55673-170-1   PRINTED IN U.S.A.

Introduction

Ever wonder how the word of Jesus' death was communicated to his many followers? This ecumenical Good Friday worship service was built around the concept that such an important event as Jesus' crucifixion would surely prompt an observer to write a letter to an acquaintance about what he or she had seen, heard, felt, and understood. This is the premise upon which our small ecumenical pastors' group based its joint Good Friday observance. We first read the Scripture passages about the crucifixion. Then each pastor chose a person who would have been near the Cross and individually expanded upon the possibilities, in the form of a letter. These we brought back another day and read to each other for comments. We found the opportunity to discuss the Scriptures with such detail and depth, in our ecumenical setting, very stimulating and invigorating.

May you find the performance of the same equally enjoyable.

Pastor Paul Weckle

The Order of Worship

Introit

Responsive Call to Worship *(Isaiah 53:1-6)*

Leader: Who has believed what we have heard? And to whom has the arm of the Lord been revealed?

People: **For he grew up before him like a young plant, and like a root out of dry ground;**

Leader: He had no form or comeliness that we should look at him, and no beauty that we should desire him.

People: **He was despised and rejected by men; a man of sorrows, and acquainted with grief;**

Leader: And as one from whom men hide their faces he was despised, and we esteemed him not.

People: **Surely he has borne our griefs and carried our sorrows; yet we esteemed him stricken, smitten by God, and afflicted.**

Leader: But he was wounded for our transgressions, he was bruised for our iniquities,

People: **Upon him was the chastisement that made us whole, and with his stripes we are healed.**

Leader: All we like sheep have gone astray, we have turned every one to his own way;

People: **And the Lord has laid on him the iniquity of us all. Amen**

Hymn: "The Old Rugged Cross"

Narrator: The following letters were composed from the viewpoint of persons who saw the crucifixion of Jesus, and who might have tried to tell a friend what they had seen and felt on that day. So, we would like to share with you the following three letters, inviting you to imagine that you have just received these very special letters from a very special friend.

Hymn: "Were you There?" *(v. 1)*

Scripture: *John 19:17-18*

"The Beloved Disciple"   by Pastor Dan and
                                              Mrs. Annette Thompson

Mother Dear,

I am feeling so confused and upset I just had to write you. For the past three years everything was so wonderful, but now it seems like the whole world has turned upside down. I don't know what to do.

Three years ago James and I were fishing with Father as we always had. I would have done that all my life if Jesus hadn't come. He said to us, "Follow me and I will make you fishers of men." It was hard for Father to understand and even harder for James and me to explain, but we had to follow him. He was what we were looking for before we knew we were looking.

Jesus. I want to describe him to you, explain my feelings, yet I'm not sure I understand it all myself. He was not a common, ordinary man. He spoke with such authority, and people listened so intently. The things he said! He called himself The Bread, The Door, The Light of the World, The Truth, The Way, The Resurrection and The Life, The Son of God, The Messiah! I was so certain that was the truth — but now I'm not sure of anything.

8

He did things I can only describe as miracles. Once we went to a wedding and when they ran out of wine he created more from mere water. The people were amazed at the quality. Another time, after a teaching session in the country, he took five loaves and two fishes and fed thousands of people. He even walked on water! It was as if all creation were under his power.

His love for people was more intense than any I've ever seen. He loved those that hated him and those that no one loves. In his love he touched the blind and they saw, the deaf and they heard, and the lame and they walked again! Once he even raised a man from the dead! I don't understand why anyone would have wanted to kill Jesus!

Yesterday we all had supper together. It was so special. Although Judas left early, the rest of us lingered a long time after the Passover meal. I felt so restful and contented inside. Later we went to the garden to pray. It was there the nightmare began.

The soldiers came and took him away. He wouldn't let us fight, and when they tried to recognize us we got so scared we ran and hid. The next day they brought him out into the courtyard. His back was bloody and bruised. His beard was splotched and bloody from where they had pulled out clumps, and his face was swollen from the beatings. As they continued calling him names, spitting on him, and pushing down on the crown of thorns my heart fell. I don't understand why he didn't stop them. He didn't even struggle.

They nailed him to a Cross and hung him between two criminals. He talked to them from there; again that love! He could have caused the earth to shake him down or angels to rescue him, but he just stayed there. I thought he even looked like he wanted to be there, but that can't be — no one would want that. When he looked at me I felt near death myself — such pain I saw him suffer, such agony I felt as I watched!

Then he died. Even though the soldier pierced his side and the water and blood flowed out when they took him down from the Cross, I couldn't take my eyes off him. I just couldn't let it be true. But as they roll the stone in place, even as I write, I know it is true. He is dead. It is all over. So what does this all mean?

Your Son, John

Hymn: "Were you There?" *(v. 2)*

Scripture: *Luke 23:33-38, 44-47*

A Soldier's Letter" by Pastor Paul J. Weckle

My dearest Penelope,

I am not used to writing, as you are well aware. I am humbled even more when I think of these words that I am about to write to you. I thought that I was beyond feeling and pain, as my job here in Palestine has been so very brutal. But today, today, I have found something for which I am not hardened. Today I had to crucify an innocent man. But it was more than his simple innocence that has me all astir. I have undoubtedly killed more innocents than this singular man. (This surprizing man, this more than man . . . this . . . man.) Today I did my duty and smashed the spike through hands and feet. All three, two criminals and this other one called Jesus, yielded to the force of the hammer . . . as they all must. I tell you Penelope, I thought I was toughened to the job which I have had to do for so long. But not anymore. Today

I killed someone who should not have been raised on the tree. I know that I did not sentence this man, Pilate did that, yet because it was my hammer that made the holes, I feel guilty.

Let me tell you what happened. Word had come from the palace that this Jesus was a revolutionary and needed to be stopped. So, Pilate sent him with two other criminals to die on the cross. I did my job. I always do. I raised him high in the sky. But this man . . . this man surprized me. He never cried out. He never flinched. He seemed to gaze caringly at me, as if to say he forgave me for hurting him. As the day went on, the usual crowd of onlookers had to be kept back, so many wanted to be near him. One time this Jesus spoke with the other criminals; to one he said, "today you will be with me in paradise." The sky grew dark, then the earth shook below my feet and suddenly the quiet Jesus cried out, "Father, into thy hands I commit my spirit!" And having said this he breathed his last.

I could not help myself — his innocence glared before me — I couldn't help it, for I said there in front of all those strangers . . . "Certainly this man was innocent."

My hands feel dirty, my world is jumping out of my control. I was able to resist for so long, but now I have gone too far. I have killed more than an innocent man. He had such stature . . . he even said to me, "Father, forgive them, for they know not what they do." I think he meant what he said, and it seemed to be not just for me but for others as well. A dying, crucified man pleading with his father to forgive us. His father?

Today, more has happened to me than all my previous years put together. And I don't understand it. The only thing I know is this: this Jesus was innocent, and this son asked his father to forgive his killers.

What have I done? I should have been saving such men as this . . . we need his kind. We needed him. I needed him. What have I done, what have I done?

Yours, Antonius

Hymn: "Were you There?" *(v. 3)*

Scripture: *Luke 23:26-28*

*"**Through A Child's Eye**"* by Father Frank DVorak

Dear Caleb,

How are you? I am fine. I hope you are fine, too. I really miss you. We had so much fun last summer. Remember all the things we did? That was always fun going into the countryside or playing down in the area outside the temple. That is part of the reason why I am writing this now. Remember that time last summer when we were playing by the temple and that man, he was called Jesus, asked me to come over to him and some other men with him, and after I got there he said to the others that they had to be like us kids or they could not get anywhere in his Kingdom? or remember that other time when we were coming back from a day of fishing and you had some bread left and I was carrying our fish and we stopped to listen to that same man as he was talking to all those people on the hillside south of town? You'll never believe what happened this past week. Sunday there was this big parade of people that came past our house — they were all carrying branches and were shouting some kind of honor to this same Jesus as he was riding a donkey. It was kind of awesome. I had not seen anything like that for a long time. Then two nights ago Dad came home and said that there was some kind of excitement going on at the praetorium — I snuck out later. I couldn't get in to see what was happening, but I came upon a group around a fire outside and some of the group was really picking on one of the men — remember that man who hollared at us that one time when we and a bunch of others wanted to get an autograph from Jesus? Wasn't his name Peter? Strange man. You know what, I heard him deny that he even knew Jesus now — boy, grownups sure are strange. Why would he deny his best friend? I'll try to keep the rest short. Yesterday this mob of people went by shouting, "crucify him." I couldn't see who it was, but from the way they were treating him, I was certain that he had to have done something serious. They were inhuman in the way they treated him. I could hear them nail his hands and feet — what pain. It wasn't until they lifted him on the Cross that I saw it was this same Jesus. I can't understand how such a good man could have died such a horrible death. Dad says that it was all a political plot. It was truly gruesome. After he died, his friends buried him and Pilate placed a detachment of soldiers to guard his tomb — I can't imagine what could happen now that he is dead.

The events of this past week are things I will long remember and I will fill you in on all the gory details when we get together again this summer — there is so much I had to skip over. Take care till then.

Your Friend, Samuel

Hymn: "Were you There?" *(v. 4)*

Prayer

Offering / Offertory

Hymn: "Beneath The Cross of Jesus"

13

Benediction:

Today is dark and dreary. Death has claimed the only sign of hope to enter our lives. On Friday's side of the Cross there is no peace, there is only sadness. Let us go forth now, remembering the darkness of that day and quietly awaiting the dawn of a new day on Easter morn. Let us go forth. Amen

Postlude

[An alternative to the above order of worship would be to mail the letters in a newsletter to the congregation members and introduce them as an additional spiritual tool in their Lenten journey. Or, one could use a letter each week for Lenten / Vesper services and encourage the participants to compose their own letters in response to each letter. Lastly, invite families to read the letters at home, then bring their own written replies to worship to be included in a service / read / shared.]